CALIFORNIA

ALASKA

CANADA

PACIFIC
OCEAN

UNITED
STATES

HAWAII

PUERTO
RICO

MEXICO

CALIFORNIA

HELLO
U.S.A.

by Kathy Pelta

Lerner Publications Company

You'll find this picture of California poppies at the beginning of each chapter in this book. These golden flowers bloom on hillsides all over the state. The California poppy was chosen as the official state flower in 1903. Every year on April 6, Californians celebrate Poppy Day.

Cover (left): Golden Gate Bridge at dusk, San Francisco. Cover (right): Hollywood sign, Hollywood, Los Angeles. Pages 2–3: Mirror Lake in Yosemite Valley, Yosemite National Park. Page 3: Sea otter eating mussels.

This book is available in two editions:
Library binding by Lerner Publications Company, a division of Lerner Publishing Group
Soft cover by First Avenue Editions, an imprint of Lerner Publishing Group
241 First Avenue North
Minneapolis, MN 55401 U.S.A.

Website address: www.lernerbooks.com

Library of Congress Cataloging-in-Publication Data

Pelta, Kathy.
   California / by Kathy Pelta (Rev. and expanded 2nd ed.)
     p.   cm. — (Hello U.S.A.)
   Includes index.
   ISBN: 0–8225–4062–2 (lib. bdg. : alk. paper)
   ISBN: 0–8225–4146–7 (pbk. : alk. paper)
   1. California—Juvenile literature. 2. California—Geography—Juvenile literature. [1. California.] I. Title. II. Series.
F861.3 .P45 2002
979.4—dc21   2001002448

Manufactured in the United States of America
1 2 3 4 5 6 – JR – 07 06 05 04 03 02

CONTENTS

Big Sur coast in Monterey County, central California. California's coastline stretches about 900 miles along the Pacific Ocean.

The Golden State

 olden poppies carpet California's meadows in spring. Each summer, grassy hills turn golden brown. Golden sunshine beams in much of the state year-round. No wonder California is called the Golden State. The Golden State also has jagged mountains, sun-baked **deserts,** cool redwood forests, and miles and miles of sandy beaches.

California's beaches line the Pacific Ocean, which borders the state on the west. The state's coast stretches from Oregon in the north all the way to Mexico in the south, a distance of about 900 miles. California's neighbors to the east are Arizona, which lies across the Colorado River, and Nevada.

In California's desert areas, the sun shines hot and strong.

7

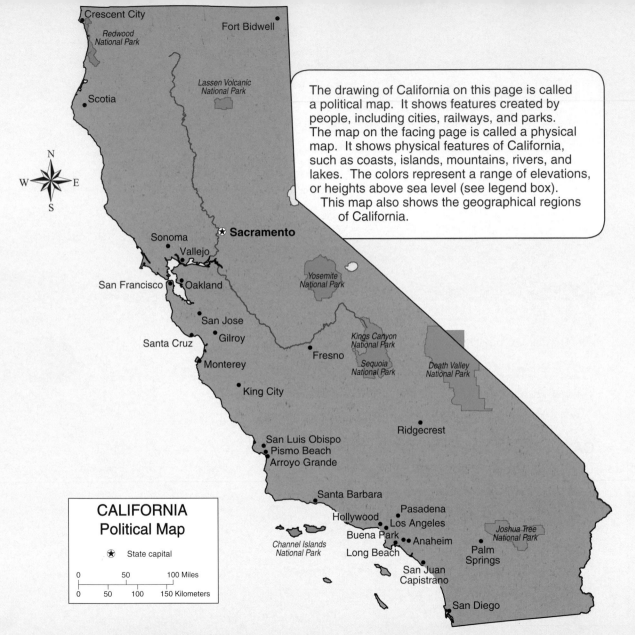

Crescent City
Fort Bidwell

Redwood National Park

Lassen Volcanic National Park

Scotia

The drawing of California on this page is called a political map. It shows features created by people, including cities, railways, and parks. The map on the facing page is called a physical map. It shows physical features of California, such as coasts, islands, mountains, rivers, and lakes. The colors represent a range of elevations, or heights above sea level (see legend box).

This map also shows the geographical regions of California.

Sonoma

⭐ **Sacramento**

Vallejo

Yosemite National Park

San Francisco
Oakland

San Jose
Gilroy

Santa Cruz

Kings Canyon National Park

Monterey

Fresno

Sequoia National Park

Death Valley National Park

King City

San Luis Obispo
Pismo Beach
Arroyo Grande

Ridgecrest

Santa Barbara

Pasadena

Hollywood
Los Angeles
Buena Park
Anaheim

Joshua Tree National Park

Channel Islands National Park

Long Beach

Palm Springs

San Juan Capistrano

San Diego

CALIFORNIA
Political Map

⭐ State capital

0	50	100 Miles

0	50	100	150 Kilometers

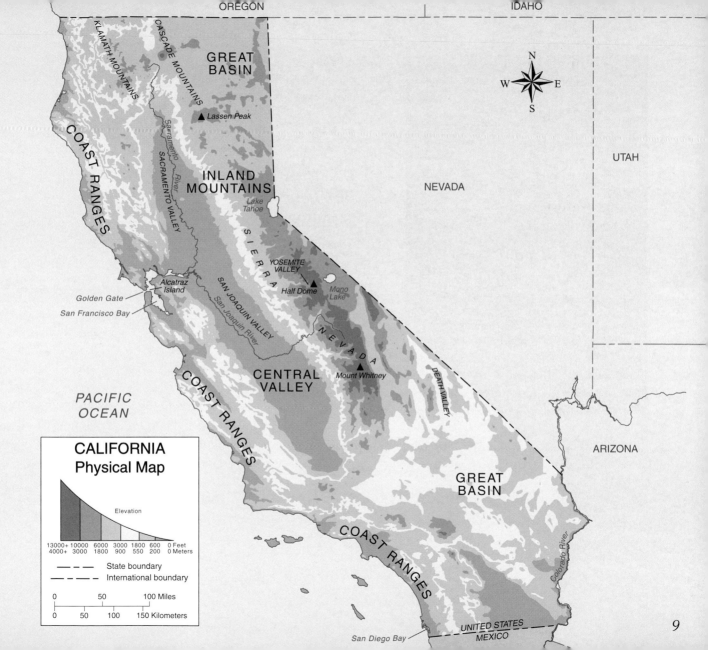

OREGON

IDAHO

KLAMATH MOUNTAINS

CASCADE MOUNTAINS

GREAT
BASIN

▲ Lassen Peak

INLAND
MOUNTAINS

COAST RANGES

Sacramento River

SACRAMENTO VALLEY

NEVADA

UTAH

Lake
Tahoe

S I E R R A

Golden Gate

Alcatraz
Island

San Francisco Bay

SAN JOAQUIN VALLEY

San Joaquin River

YOSEMITE
VALLEY

Half Dome ▲

Mono
Lake

N E V A D A

Mount Whitney ▲

CENTRAL
VALLEY

DEATH VALLEY

PACIFIC
OCEAN

COAST RANGES

ARIZONA

GREAT
BASIN

COAST RANGES

Colorado River

CALIFORNIA
Physical Map

Elevation

13000+ 10000 6000 3000 1800 600 0 Feet
4000+ 3000 1800 900 550 200 0 Meters

– – – State boundary

– · – International boundary

0   50   100 Miles

0   50   100   150 Kilometers

San Diego Bay

UNITED STATES
MEXICO

N
W E
S

9

Lassen Peak, an active volcano in the Cascade Mountains, is made up of lava formations.

California can be divided into four geographic regions. They are the Coast Ranges, the Inland Mountains, the Central Valley, and the Great Basin. The Coast Ranges stretch the entire length of California along the Pacific Ocean. Most of the mountains in these ranges are low, but some peaks of the Klamath Mountains in the north reach up to 8,000 feet.

The Inland Mountains also run north and south. Their two major ranges—the Cascade Mountains and the Sierra Nevada—contain some of the highest peaks in the United States, including Mount Whitney at 14,494 feet. Volcanoes created the Cascades millions of years ago, when fiery melted rock called lava oozed out of the earth's crust and hardened into mountains.

Half Dome *(left)*, a peak in the Sierra Nevada, overlooks Yosemite Valley. The landscape around Mono Lake *(above)*, located high in the Sierra Nevada, looks like the moon. Calcium deposits give the rocks their white coating and spirelike shapes.

11

Long ago, huge bodies of ice known as **glaciers** moved slowly over the high parts of the Sierra Nevada and carved deep canyons. Later the glaciers melted, creating hundreds of streams and lakes, including Lake Tahoe.

California's long, flat Central Valley separates the Coast Ranges from the Inland Mountains. Fertile soil has made the Central Valley the state's best farmland. Two of the state's major rivers—the Sacramento and the San Joaquin—flow through the

California's Central Valley is home to lush farmland.

California deserts include all kinds of landscapes, such as cracked mud, sand dunes, and rocky mountains.

region. These waterways join near the capital city of Sacramento and together flow west into San Francisco Bay. From there, a **strait** (water passageway) called the Golden Gate leads to the Pacific Ocean.

In the Great Basin, California's driest region, soil cracks from lack of rain. **Irrigation,** a method of watering land, allows farmers to work dry land in some areas. But in most of the region, vast deserts stretch for miles. One area of the Great Basin is so hot and dry it was named Death Valley to warn travelers to stay away.

Death Valley is a place of great natural beauty and dangerously high temperatures.

Death Valley once recorded a scorching temperature of 134° F. Summer highs of 120° F are normal for California's inland valleys, but winters bring freezing temperatures. Along the northern coast, people shiver during cool, foggy summers and rainy, cold winters, but autumns are warm and sunny. Southern Californians enjoy mild temperatures, sea breezes, and sunshine most of the year.

No matter where people live in the state, they can divide the year into two seasons—one dry and one wet. From May to October, it rarely rains anywhere. In the winter, rain falls mostly in the north, and snow covers the mountains. Annual rainfall varies from 2 inches in desert areas to 100 inches along the northern coast.

Low rainfall can be a serious threat. Another threat is earthquakes. Most earthquakes are small and cause no damage, but major quakes can topple buildings, bridges, and freeways in a few seconds. Earthquakes occur along **fault lines,** where sections of the earth's crust meet and rub against each other, causing the earth to shake. The longest fault in the state, the San Andreas Fault, extends from northern California to Mexico.

A devastating earthquake ripped through San Francisco in 1906. The tremor lasted only 90 seconds, but the fires it caused burned for three days.

The Shasta Dam and Reservoir *(above)* show the effects of a drought.

Who Gets the Water?

Californians depend on the rain and snow that fall during the wet season to provide them with water all year long. To store water, the state has built reservoirs, or artificial lakes. Falling rain and melting snow fill mountain streams that flow into the reservoirs. Then aqueducts, or canals, carry the water to all parts of the state.

When rainfall is lower than usual, the reservoirs can't provide enough water to go around, and everyone must help to conserve it. By law, more than half of California's water goes to farmers. Yet urban areas, especially in the south, keep growing and needing more water. This leads to one of the state's biggest problems—who gets the water? The question has no easy answers, and the debate continues.

Colorful iguanas live in the deserts of California.

Like landforms and climates in California, a wide variety of animals and plants exist in the state. Rattlesnakes, lizards, and tortoises rest in the shade of desert cacti, while bighorn sheep climb among bristlecone pines in the high country.

The condor, which is nearly extinct, is the largest flying bird in North America. With a wingspan of more than eight feet, it soars over scrub oaks in the foothills of southern California. Peregrine falcons nest in the rocky cliffs of Yosemite National Park in the Sierra Nevada.

Mountain lions live
in many parts
of California.

    California's state animal, the grizzly bear, no
longer inhabits the Golden State, but black bears
still roam the mountains. Cougars and mountain
lions prey on the many deer that thrive throughout
the state. Sea lions play on rocky coasts. Elephant
seals bask in the sun on sandy beaches. Whales
swim offshore and occasionally pass through the
Golden Gate into San Francisco Bay!

Missions, Mines, and Movies

bout 12,000 years ago, the first people to come to the California area arrived from the north and the east. Over many centuries, groups struggled across the rugged mountains and vast deserts that form California's borders. Descendants of these people are called American Indians, or Native Americans.

Somewhere between 200 and 500 different Indian nations, or tribes, eventually settled in California. Each nation spoke its own language and had its own way of life.

Cave paintings like this one were left behind by the Chumash.

19

The nations of the southern coast were among the largest. Some villages built by the Chumash Indians had more than 1,000 people. Skilled fishers from several nations traveled the sea in oceangoing canoes, gathering shellfish and other sea creatures for food.

To the north, abundant plant and animal life provided plenty of food. In the central part of California, the most important food source was the acorn, which comes from oak trees. Using stones, women pounded dried acorns into powder to make cakes or boiled cereal similar to oatmeal.

Available building materials and local climates determined how the Indians built their homes. Miwok people in Yosemite Valley built their lodges with thick slabs of bark from local forests.

Native American Nations in California

The Native Americans of California can be divided into six regions, or culture areas. The lifestyles of these people varied greatly, because the climate, plants, and animals were so different in each area. Within each area were several distinct tribes, or nations. This map shows the six culture areas and a few of the hundreds of Indian nations within California.

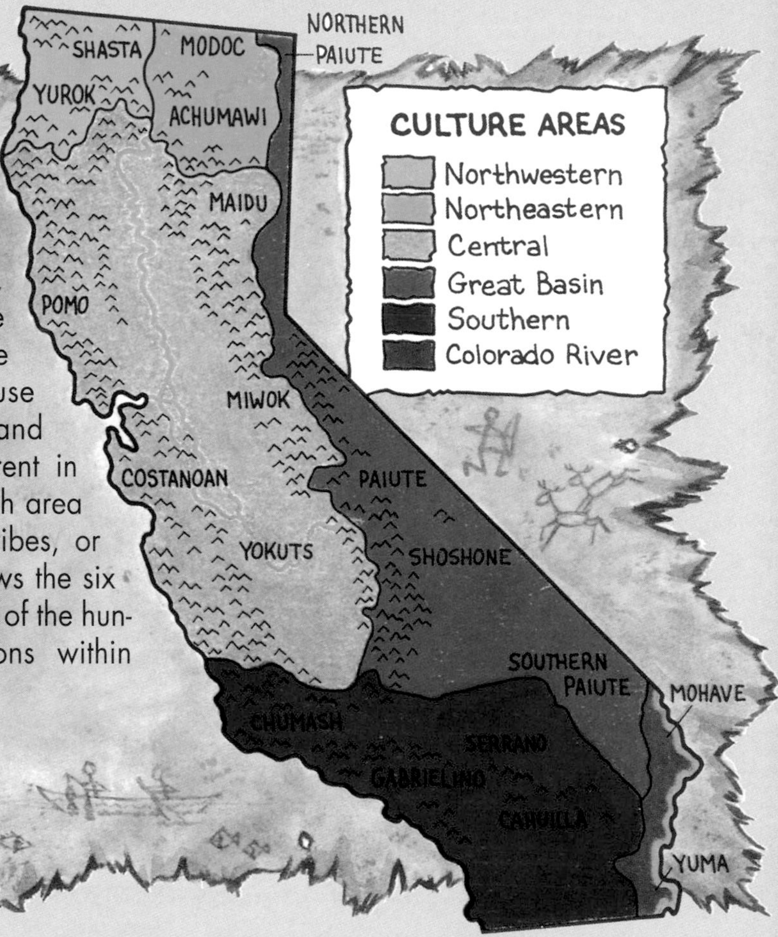

CULTURE AREAS
- Northwestern
- Northeastern
- Central
- Great Basin
- Southern
- Colorado River

SHASTA
MODOC
NORTHERN PAIUTE
YUROK
ACHUMAWI
MAIDU
POMO
MIWOK
COSTANOAN
PAIUTE
YOKUTS
SHOSHONE
SOUTHERN PAIUTE
MOHAVE
CHUMASH
SERRANO
GABRIELINO
CAHUILLA
YUMA

The Maidu, who lived in the Sacramento Valley, covered their homes with dirt and clay to keep out the sun's heat.

Central nations each had several villages scattered far apart, giving villagers enough space to hunt and gather food. Trespassing was usually forbidden, so members of a nation had little contact with neighboring communities. Each village had a leader to give advice, and men and women called shamans performed religious ceremonies. In ceremonies to cure illness, the shaman danced or sang, blew smoke on the part that hurt, or tried to suck out the source of pain.

In the Klamath Mountains to the north, the Indians

shared some customs with those of central peoples. Food, clothing, and the use of shamans were similar. But northern nations valued possessions more than their southern neighbors did. The richest men— those who had the most woodpecker scalps, white deerskins, and seashells—were the leaders.

Along the eastern strip of what became California, dry weather made food and water scarce. The Indians in this area had to spend most of their time searching for food. Life along the Colorado River in the southeast was a little easier. Here, the Indians channeled water from the river to grow crops such as corn, beans, and pumpkins. The southeastern nations were the most organized peoples of the region. They united to fight wars, and they traveled far to trade with other nations.

Indians in California probably never saw a white person until the mid-1500s. At that time, Spaniards in search of gold found what they thought was an island near the west coast of Mexico. They called the island California, after a treasure island they had read about in a book.

However, this part of Mexico, called Baja (Lower) California, turned out to be a **peninsula,** not an island. And it had no treasure. So the king of Spain sent Juan Rodríguez Cabrillo north to explore the region beyond Baja California. In 1542 Cabrillo sailed into San Diego Bay, becoming the first European to visit Alta (Upper) California. Finding no gold, he soon left.

The next European visitor, England's Sir Francis Drake, did not stay long either. In 1579 his ship stopped north of the site that later became San Francisco. He claimed the land for his country's queen. Drake then sailed home, never to return.

During a stop near San Francisco Bay, Francis Drake met coastal Indians.

Some of the Spanish guards who ran the presidios treated Indian workers like slaves.

For nearly 200 years after that, the Indians in California lived undisturbed by outsiders. Mountains, deserts, and the ocean isolated them from other people.

In 1769 Spain acted to secure its claim to this land. Spanish soldiers built a presidio, or fort, in the area that later became San Diego. Father Junípero Serra and some other Catholic priests from Spain set up a **mission** there. Within 40 years, 4 presidios and 21 missions dotted the California coast.

The missions were part church and part pueblo, or town. Father Serra's plan was to teach coastal Indians the Catholic religion. He also taught them how to make adobe (clay) bricks and how to irrigate fields, tend crops, and raise cattle.

Some missions, such as Santa Barbara, eventually expanded into thriving cities.

But the Spaniards weren't without competition. Russian fur traders established Fort Ross on the northwestern California coast in 1812. The Russians stayed at the fort for 20 years, making money on sea otter pelts, before leaving the area.

Meanwhile, the Spanish missions continued to operate. The mission Indians grew food and raised animals, but they were forced to work and to worship. They had to give up their old ways of life, their own foods, and their traditional religions. Many tried to run away, only to be captured and flogged or put in chains as a warning to others.

Within a few years, thousands of Indians who lived at the missions died from European diseases such as measles and smallpox. When the Spaniards first arrived, 300,000 Indians lived in California. By the time Mexico won its independence from Spain in 1821, fewer than 150,000 Indians remained. The next year, California became part of Mexico.

As an independent nation, Mexico ended the mission system. Much of the missionary land was divided into large estates called ranchos.

Although Spanish officials had promised land to the Indians, they gave most of the land to Mexican settlers. Most of these settlers were descendants of the Spanish people. With no property of their own, many Indians were stuck working on the ranchos for little or no money.

Unlike Spain, Mexico allowed outsiders to come to its territories. Trading ships from the East Coast of the United States docked at California's ports to load cowhides and animal furs. U.S. trappers blazed mountain trails to the West Coast, and pioneers soon followed in covered wagons. The first party to travel to California by land arrived in 1841. Still, by 1845 the population of California, not including Indians, was only 7,000.

Many settlers traveled west to California by wagon train in the 1800s.

Disaster at Donner Pass

During the 1840s, pioneers began moving west to California. The journey was long and difficult. Stretches of desert and steep, rocky mountains were especially hard to cross.

In 1846 a group of families from Illinois organized by George Donner loaded their wagons and headed west. By the time the Donner party reached Wyoming, they were already behind schedule. When they heard of a shortcut across Utah, they decided to try their luck.

Unfortunately, the Donner party soon discovered that the shortcut actually took longer because it was so treacherous. By the time the group reached the top of the Sierra Nevada in early November of 1846, a snowstorm had made crossing the mountains impossible.

The Donner party realized they would have to settle in for the winter. They quickly made makeshift cabins. As food ran short, the pioneers struggled to find anything to eat—twigs, mice, their dogs, shoes. People grew weak and sick. Some died.

By mid-December, they decided to send 17 people ahead to try and get help. Half died of cold and starvation, and it was more than a month before one member reached a town. Rescue teams with food set out in February of 1847.

Meanwhile, food grew even scarcer in the mountain camp. As cold and hunger made the survivors more and more desperate, they were forced to cook and eat the bodies of people who had died.

By the time the rescue team finally arrived, almost half of the 87 members of the Donner party had died. In memory of the tragedy, the path they took over the mountains is named Donner Pass *(pictured above).*

In 1846 Captain John C. Frémont of the U.S. Army arrived in California. When a band of American settlers made plans for California to break away from Mexico, Frémont helped them. On June 14, 1846, the men stormed Sonoma presidio and hoisted a homemade flag painted with a grizzly bear and the words "California Republic." The action was known as the Bear Flag Revolt.

About one month before, in May 1846, the United States and Mexico had gone to war over a border dispute. Most of the fighting took place in Texas. In California, Mexican soldiers surrendered after a few skirmishes. When the Mexican War ended, California became a U.S. territory.

The peace **treaty** that ended the Mexican War was signed on February 2, 1848. Only days before, an amazing discovery had been made at Sutter's sawmill in the foothills east of Sacramento. James Marshall, an American working at the mill, saw something shining in a stream. It was gold!

Mill workers tried to keep the discovery secret. But word quickly leaked out—and the gold rush was on. Adventurers from all over the world headed for California. By 1849, 40,000 gold seekers—nicknamed forty-niners after the year in which they came—were swarming over the gold-rich country. That year they took out $30 million worth of nuggets and gold dust.

When gold was discovered at Sutter's Mill *(left)*, thousands of people flocked to California to try to strike it rich.

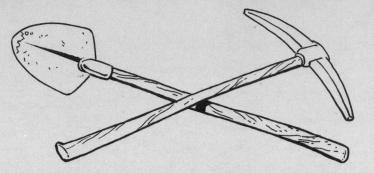

African Americans and the Gold Rush

Among the many newcomers to California during the gold rush were African Americans. Some were slaves who came from Southern states to work in the mines and use their earnings to buy their freedom. Moses Rodgers, for example, worked his way out of slavery and gained fame as one of the best mining engineers in California. Many black miners saved money to free relatives still held as slaves in the South.

Some black newcomers became rich by providing services to the gold diggers. Some set up shops. Mifflin Gibbs was one of the owners of the only shoe store in San Francisco during the gold rush. George Dennis rented a gambling table at the Eldorado Hotel in San Francisco. His mother used the table to sell hot meals to gamblers at huge profits.

With many goods in short supply, prices were sky high. Shopkeepers could sell an apple or an egg for one dollar. A loaf of bread was 10 times the usual price, and medicine was $10 a pill. Some African Americans bought land cheaply and made a fortune selling it at much higher prices a few years later.

With wealth so easy to come by, a person's history or skin color didn't matter. San Francisco, a gateway to the gold country, became the state's largest city, bustling with bankers, traders, and merchants of all colors.

While the forty-niners were digging for gold, a group of lawmakers met in Monterey to write a constitution, or basic set of laws, for California. The constitution forbade slavery, but it also mirrored the U.S. Constitution by not allowing blacks, Native Americans, and women the right to vote. California's white males—the only people who could vote—approved the constitution in 1849. And on September 9, 1850, California became the 31st state in the Union.

By 1860 California's population had swelled to 300,000. But the number of Indians had dwindled to barely 30,000. Most had died from diseases brought by newcomers.

To many Americans, gold had made California seem like the land of their dreams. But getting there wasn't easy. By ship, a journey from the East Coast could last up to four months. From the Midwest, the trip by stagecoach took 20 days.

To make travel easier, four Californians decided to build a railroad. This new railroad would hook up with tracks being laid from the East Coast.

At this rally, the Big Four and other Californians celebrated the groundbreaking for the Central Pacific Railroad. The railway brought wealth to the four men. They used some of the money to bribe, or pay, lawmakers to vote for laws that helped the railroad business.

In 1861 these businessmen—Leland Stanford, Mark Hopkins, Charles Crocker, and Collis P. Huntington, known as the Big Four—formed the Central Pacific Company.

To solve the problem of finding workers, the Big Four brought 10,000 laborers from China to lay the tracks. By 1869 the eastern and western branches of the railroad met in Utah. With a silver hammer, officials drove in the final spike—made of California gold.

After the railroad was finished, it took only seven

days to make the journey from New York to California. No longer would deserts and mountains isolate the state from the rest of the nation.

Meanwhile, Chinese workers began to compete with Americans for other jobs. The Chinese were willing to work for very low pay. White workers protested, crying, "California for Americans!" In 1882 the U.S. Congress passed a law to stop Chinese **immigrants** from coming.

Chinese workers built many of the railroad tracks in the state of California.

At the same time, California businesspeople were urging vacationers to come to the Golden State to improve their health in the sunny climate of southern California. Railroads lured people west with cheap train tickets. Landholders in Los Angeles grew rich selling land to the new arrivals.

In the early 1900s, California attracted moviemakers, too. Besides sunny skies all year, southern California had a variety of background scenery—from deserts and cattle ranches to mountains and

Many people who hoped to act in glamorous Hollywood movies moved to the Golden State.

the seashore. Hollywood, a district in Los Angeles, soon became the motion-picture capital of the world.

While the south thrived, an earthquake rocked San Francisco in 1906, killing at least 3,000 people and destroying about 28,000 buildings. The city was rebuilt soon after.

Many people attracted by the movie industry found jobs in other new and growing industries. This was especially true during the 1920s, when a different type of gold—black gold, or oil—was discovered at three different sites near Los Angeles.

By this time, many Americans owned cars and needed gasoline (which is made from oil) to fuel their vehicles. Oil soon became Los Angeles's most important industry. Within a few years, the city passed San Francisco as California's largest urban area.

The 1906 San Francisco earthquake destroyed thousands of buildings in the city.

Since Los Angeles lay in a desert, the city had to pipe in water from the north. But with thousands of newcomers arriving each year, the city did not have enough water. In 1928 workers began building a dam across the Colorado River to collect more water. The dam permanently flooded land in the area, and hundreds of people lost their property.

Despite this sign of progress, the Great Depression, a major slump in the nation's economy, struck in 1929. Businesses failed. Tourists no longer came to California to spend money. Instead, jobless people flowed into the state, spurred by rumors of jobs. Many of the people were migrant workers, who moved from place to place to find jobs picking fruit and vegetables.

California's businesses finally began to boom in 1941, when the United

This famous photograph was taken by Dorothea Lange during the depression. This migrant worker has just sold the tires off the family's car to buy food.

Due to wartime prejudices, thousands of Japanese Americans were forced to live in camps from 1942 to 1944.

States entered World War II (1939–1945). Thousands of Americans in California's shipyards and defense plants built ships and planes for the war. Navy vessels swarmed in the harbors. Soldiers trained at camps around the state.

While California geared up for war, some people worried that Japanese Americans living in the state might be spies for enemy countries, which included Japan. In 1942 the U.S. government forced 93,000 Japanese Americans in California to abandon their homes and move to inland camps. The prisoners were not allowed to leave the camps until late 1944.

During and after the war, people again moved west to California. Many soldiers who had been stationed in California brought their families to settle there. Thousands of African Americans moved to California to take jobs in factories. And new laws allowed more Asian and **Latino** immigrants into California.

Of all the different groups in California, African Americans became the most active in a movement for equality. They wanted the same chances for good housing, jobs, and schools that white Californians had.

Tension increased between white and black neighborhoods. In 1965 riots broke out in Watts, a black district in Los Angeles. Nearly 30 years later, in 1992, riots again broke out in Los Angeles when a California jury found four white policemen not guilty in the beating of Rodney King, a black motorist.

With almost 34 million people, California has other problems. Schools in many urban areas are overcrowded. More and more cars clog the freeways and pollute the air. In addition, California's energy

Rioting in Watts in 1965 caused fires, which destroyed several buildings.

resources cannot always keep up with the demand. In 2000 and 2001, parts of the state suffered blackouts—periods without electrical power.

Newcomers continue to flood into the state. At the same time, some Californians have chosen to leave for states with better job opportunities. For some, the Golden State may have lost its glitter. But for many others, it's a chance at a new beginning. Californians continue working to build a better future for their state.

PEOPLE & ECONOMY

A Diverse Workforce

alifornia's state motto—Eureka—is a Greek word that means "I've found it." In 1849 the forty-niners found gold. The pioneers who followed them west found hope and a chance to start a new life. Since California joined the Union in 1850, many more people have flocked to the state. In fact, California's 33.9 million residents make it by far the most populous state in the country.

More and more immigrants—mainly from Mexico, Central and South America, and Southeast Asia— are looking for a new beginning in the Golden State. In fact, about one out of every five people living in California was born in another country.

Almost one in three Californians has Latin

American roots. Some of these Latinos are descendants of the Mexicans who lived in California when it was still part of Mexico. The 3.8 million people from Asia and the Pacific Islands represent about 11 percent of California's population. More than 2 million African Americans live in the state.

Few of California's original American Indian nations have survived. Most of the Indians living in California came from other states. The population numbers about 179,000—fewer than 1 percent of all Californians. Some Indians live on reservations, or lands set aside for them by the U.S. government.

People from many places make up California's large population.

Only 5 percent of Californians live in rural areas. The rest live in cities and suburbs, mostly near the coast. In the south are California's largest cities—Los Angeles with about 3.7 million people and San Diego with more than 1.2 million. Clustered in the San Francisco Bay area, the main cities in the north are San Jose, San Francisco, and Oakland. The fastest growing communities in the Central Valley are Fresno and Sacramento, the state capital.

Cities both north and south have art galleries, museums, theater groups, and symphony

Sacramento, the state capital, has over 400,000 residents.

The Paramount Theatre in Oakland was built in 1931. It features music, dance, and movies.

orchestras. San Francisco also boasts well-known opera and ballet companies.

Since the first movies were made in Hollywood in the early 1900s, southern California has been the film capital of the world. Over the years, radio, television, and music recording have also become big businesses in California, entertaining millions of people worldwide.

California is a sports lover's dream. Professional teams include basketball's Los Angeles Lakers, Sacramento Kings, Los Angeles Clippers, and Golden State Warriors. The Anaheim Mighty Ducks, Los Angeles Kings, and San Jose Sharks play hockey. California has five professional baseball teams—the Oakland A's, Los Angeles Dodgers, San Diego Padres, San Francisco Giants, and Anaheim Angels.

In football, the Oakland Raiders, the San Diego Chargers, and the San Francisco 49ers all battle for their shot at the Super Bowl.

For recreation, many Californians head outdoors. At lakes and ocean beaches, people fish, surf, sail, water-ski, and scuba dive. Campers can hike in one of California's many national, state, and county parks. In the winter, skiers swoosh down the snowy slopes of the Sierra Nevada and the Cascades.

Nearly every weekend, a California city or town features a special event. Native Americans take part in games and traditional dances at powwows

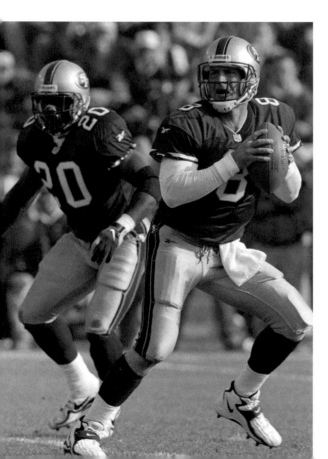

The San Francisco 49ers and their fans have enjoyed the skills of two of football's best quarterbacks— Joe Montana and Steve Young *(left, with football)*.

Fruits and vegetables are abundant in California. People celebrate at festivals honoring garlic *(right)* and asparagus *(far right)*.

and fairs. Latino communities celebrate Mexican independence with fiestas on Cinco de Mayo, which means "May 5" in Spanish. Parades with dragons and floats mark Chinese New Year in San Francisco's Chinatown. In San Jose, the Hoi Tet Festival celebrates Vietnamese New Year.

Farming communities host festivals to honor crops from artichokes to zucchini. Pismo Beach has a clam-digging competition. And at the Gilroy Garlic Festival, people can even sample garlic ice cream!

Agriculture is a major industry in California, but only 4 percent of the state's workforce have jobs on farms. California grows more than half of the nation's fruits, vegetables, and nuts. Among the leading farm products are cotton, hay, wheat, poultry, and cattle. More grapes are harvested in California than in any other state. They are sold as fresh fruit, dried to make raisins, or crushed to make wine and juice.

Two out of three workers in California hold service jobs helping people or businesses. These include jobs in California's large tourism industry. Many

California's warm, sunny climate is ideal for growing grapes *(below)* and flowers *(below right).*

Fantasy Castle at Disneyland in Anaheim is a destination for millions of tourists each year.

service workers have jobs in hotels, restaurants, resorts, or amusement parks such as Disneyland. Others work as store clerks, nurses, lawyers, or bank tellers.

Thirteen percent of California's workers have government jobs. Some government jobs are with the Forest Service, which helps manage the state's parks and forests. Wildfires that burn forests and brush and threaten homes are a serious concern to Californians during the dry season.

California's first gold rush made the state wealthy, and workers still mine more gold than in any other state except Nevada. But in modern times, oil earns the state much more money than gold does.

Fishing crews mend their nets *(above)*. Workers fix an oil drilling rig in Huntington Beach *(above right)*.

California's fishing industry operates out of harbors along the coast. Fishing crews catch shrimp, red snapper, tuna, and other fish to sell throughout the country. Very few Californians—fewer than 1 percent—work in fishing or in mining.

Loggers cut down trees from northern California's forests for the state's wood-products industry. Although lumber sales are lower than they once were, California still provides more than 10 percent of the nation's lumber.

CALIFORNIA
Economic Map

The symbols on this map show where different economic activities take place in California. The legend below explains what each symbol stands for.

Barley	Fruit	Olives
Cattle	Gold	Potatoes
Cotton	Grapes	Poultry
Dairy products	Hay	Rice
Fish	Manufacturing	Sand and gravel
Forest products	Mining	Sheep
Natural gas	Stone	
Oil	Sugar beets	
Tourism		
Vegetables		
Walnuts		

Northern towns, such as Scotia, are in the center of California's logging industry.

Factories employ 11 percent of the state's workforce, or about 1 out of every 10 workers. These men and women may be engineers, machine operators, or technicians. Many of them design and assemble aircraft, space vehicles, and communication systems at aerospace centers in southern California.

Some factories make electronic equipment and computers. Using a substance called silicon, workers build computer parts in a small area between San Jose and San Francisco. This region has come to be known as Silicon Valley.

With the growth in importance of the World Wide Web, Californians have worked to improve its services. In 1994 Jerry Yang and David Filo, two classmates at Stanford University, indexed their favorite web links to create the popular Yahoo! search engine. Many other Californians have followed their lead in Internet innovation.

With its varied goods and services, California's economy is larger than the economies of many countries. In fact, if California were a separate country, the value of its goods and services would rank among the top 10 countries in the world. Californians continue to make the most of their diverse workforce and natural resources.

Reducing Air Pollution

alifornia seems like a paradise to many people. It has mountain wildernesses and peaceful beaches. Its long dry season allows for all kinds of outdoor activities. But many Californians are concerned about a problem that threatens to spoil their paradise—air pollution.

California measures the highest levels of air pollution in the country. Most of the pollution is caused by burning **fossil fuels**—coal, oil, and natural gas—to produce energy.

Cars cause a lot of the pollution in California. Automobile engines get energy by burning gasoline, an oil product. This in turn produces car exhaust. The exhaust is made up of many gases, including carbon monoxide, nitrogen oxides, and unburned fuel.

When the unburned fuel and other gases in car exhaust combine with sunlight, the mixture causes **smog,** a hazy form of air pollution. The word "smog" is a combination of the words "smoke" and "fog."

By blocking the sun, smog creates hazy conditions in the Golden State. It slows the growth of crops and other plants. Smog also makes eyes sting and can cause serious breathing problems.

The mountains surrounding Los Angeles trap smog in the city.

Southern California's mountain ranges and climate worsen smoggy conditions. The mountains around Los Angeles trap gases in the city. Warm air and gases also become trapped in the area when weather conditions prevent the free flow of air.

One way to reduce air pollution is to make and drive vehicles designed to use fuel more efficiently. California's transportation companies are beginning to use vehicles that run on natural gas, methanol, or electricity. Experts hope that these fuels will not add as much to the smog problem.

Traffic in California's cities is a leading cause of smog.

Santa Cruz police officers save gas by riding bikes.

California requires that all vehicles driven in crowded areas be tested regularly. The tests measure the levels of smog-forming gases in the exhaust from tailpipes. In fact, California started the strictest standards in the nation for this type of testing, called emissions testing, in 1990.

The state also limits what people can burn. For example, some communities restrict the use of wood fires to reduce smoke in the air.

In some states, power plants are a big source of air pollution. Like many other states, California gets most of its electricity by burning fossil fuels. Some states burn coal. California, however, uses primarily natural gas. Natural gas is a much cleaner fuel to burn than coal is.

California leads the nation in the use of environmentally friendly power sources. Windmills supply electricity to communities.

California also generates about 40 percent of its electricity from water power, which does not pollute the air at all. Dams built across streams high in the mountains trap melting snow. The power of the water is then used to turn big engines that produce electricity. The dams also provide water for farms and households. Dams do have some drawbacks, though. They can be especially hard on local wildlife populations.

Power companies in California use other energy sources—such as windmills and nuclear power—that do not burn fossil fuels. Scientists are also developing ways to capture the energy from sunlight for use in solar power.

Buying the equipment for these new technologies is expensive, and change is slow. The use of nuclear power has also been limited because waste materials and accidents at nuclear plants can be extremely dangerous to human health if they are not handled properly.

Everyone can help with some of the solutions to air pollution. For example, every time Californians choose to walk or ride a bike instead of driving, they cut down on the amount of car exhaust in the air. Sharing rides or taking a bus or train also reduces the number of cars on the road. Through these and other efforts, Californians are doing their part to cut air pollution in the Golden State.

Fun Facts

The Golden Gate Bridge in San Francisco is one of the longest suspension bridges in the world. It spans 6,450 feet of water at the entrance to San Francisco Bay.

The biggest and oldest trees in the world grow in California. Redwoods are the tallest, sweeping the sky at more than 300 feet. Giant sequoias have trunks that measure more than 25 feet from side to side. And some bristlecone pines are more than 4,000 years old!

You can experience the shakes of an earthquake by entering artificial "safequakes" at Universal Studios in Los Angeles.

Sherman Tree, Sequoia National Park

Levi's denim jeans were first made in California in 1874. Levi Strauss made the pants tough enough to withstand hard wear by miners. He used heavy canvas with brass rivets to reinforce the seams. The jeans have been popular ever since.

Every year on March 19, people from all over the world come to San Juan Capistrano, California, to watch thousands of swallows return from their winter homes.

About 40,000 years ago, prehistoric animals became trapped in a gooey mess at the La Brea Tar Pits in Los Angeles. The animals got stuck in the murky tar that lay under a pool of water. Scientists are still digging out the remains.

STATE SONG

The words to California's state song were written by F. B. Silverwood, a Los Angeles merchant. Alfred Frankenstein, a former conductor for the Los Angeles Symphony Orchestra, later set the words to music. The song was adopted by the state legislature in 1951.

I LOVE YOU, CALIFORNIA

Music by Alfred Frankenstein, words by F. B. Silverwood

You can hear "I Love You, California" by visiting this website:
<http://www.50states.com/songs/calif.htm>

A CALIFORNIA RECIPE

California produces more than half of the nation's fruit, including strawberries, oranges, and grapes. With this recipe, you can have a healthy and sweet California experience. If you don't have strawberries, you can substitute bananas or create your own fruit combination.

CALIFORNIA SMOOTHIE

7 strawberries
8 ounces lemon yogurt
1/3 cup orange juice

1. In a plastic container, freeze strawberries for one hour.
2. Combine yogurt, orange juice, and frozen strawberries in a blender.
3. Cover and blend until mixture is smooth.
4. Serve in a tall glass.

HISTORICAL TIMELINE

10,000 B.C. Native Americans first arrive in what later became California.

A.D. 1542 Juan Rodríguez Cabrillo is the first European to visit California.

1579 Sir Francis Drake claims California for England.

1769 Junípero Serra builds California's first mission at San Diego.

1776 Spanish settlers from Mexico reach the area that would later become San Francisco.

1812 Russian fur traders build Fort Ross.

1821 Mexico wins independence from Spain.

1822 California becomes part of Mexico.

1841 The first organized group of American settlers, the Bidwell-Bartelson party, travels to California by land.

1846 American settlers take over Sonoma presidio and raise the Bear Flag.

1846–1848 The United States and Mexico fight the Mexican War, which ends with a U.S. victory; California becomes a U.S. territory.

1849 The California gold rush begins.

1850 California becomes the 31st state.

1869 Railroad tracks link California to the East Coast.

1882 Chinese immigration to the United States is stopped.

1906 A San Francisco earthquake causes fires and destroys much of the city.

1929 Migrant workers begin flooding into California during the Great Depression.

1942 Japanese Americans in California are moved to prison camps during World War II (1939–1945).

1965 The U.S. Immigration Act permits more people from Asia and Latin America to move to California; riots take place in the Watts neighborhood of Los Angeles.

1992 Riots erupt in Los Angeles in response to the Rodney King verdict.

1994 A strong earthquake hits Los Angeles.

2001 California faces an energy crisis, as electricity runs short and residents experience blackouts.

OUTSTANDING CALIFORNIANS

Ansel Adams

Ansel Adams (1902–1984), from San Francisco, was a photographer of western landscapes. He became famous for his pictures of mountains, forests, and other wilderness areas. Adams also worked to preserve the nation's wilderness.

Shirley Temple Black (born 1928), a curly-haired child superstar of the 1930s, had roles in many movies, including *Heidi* and *The Little Princess*. Born in Santa Monica, Black went on to serve as U.S. ambassador to Ghana and to Czechoslovakia.

Thomas Bradley

Thomas Bradley (1917–1998) became the first black mayor of Los Angeles in 1973. Widely supported by both African Americans and whites, he was elected to five terms in a row. In 1984 Bradley won the Spingarn Medal for his work as a lawyer and for his leadership skills.

Julia Child (born 1912) is a master of French cooking from Pasadena, California. In 1963 she hosted the first cooking television show, called *The French Chef*, for which she won an Emmy. She has written several popular cookbooks.

Natalie Cole

Natalie Cole (born 1950) is a rhythm-and-blues singer from Los Angeles. The daughter of Nat "King" Cole, Natalie Cole has won several awards, including two Grammys for her album *Inseparable*.

Leonardo DiCaprio

Leonardo DiCaprio (born 1974), an actor from Hollywood, California, got his start in the 1993 film *This Boy's Life*. His other films include *What's Eating Gilbert Grape*, for which he won an Oscar as best supporting actor; *Titanic*; *Marvin's Room*; and *The Beach*.

Joe DiMaggio (1914–1999), from Martinez, California, was one of the greatest outfielders in baseball history. He also set a major league record for the longest hitting streak, which lasted for 56 games in a row. DiMaggio, who played for the New York Yankees, was elected to the National Baseball Hall of Fame in 1955.

Joe DiMaggio

Clint Eastwood (born 1930) has starred in numerous movies, including *Dirty Harry*. Originally from San Francisco, Eastwood won an Oscar in 1993 as best director for *Unforgiven*.

Clint Eastwood

Robert Frost (1874–1963) was one of the leading American poets of the 1900s. Born in San Francisco, he was awarded the Pulitzer Prize for poetry four times. His poems are known for capturing the scenery of rural New England.

Ernest Gallo (born 1909) and **Julio Gallo** (1911–1993) were born in Modesto, California. The two brothers started making wine in 1933. Together, they built E & J Gallo into one of the nation's leading wineries.

Robert Frost

Jerry Garcia (1942–1995), from San Francisco, was the founder and lead guitarist and vocalist of the Grateful Dead. Formed in the 1960s and still popular, the band combined the sounds of bluegrass and folk music.

Martha Graham (1894–1991) was a dancer raised in Santa Barbara, California. At age 22, she began training in classical ballet. Graham soon developed her own style. She started her own school and dance company, helping shape modern dance in the 1900s.

Jerry Garcia

Merle Haggard

Merle Haggard (born 1937), a well-known country-western singer, was born in an abandoned refrigerator car in Bakersfield, California. Haggard began his singing career after his first career, as a petty thief, landed him in prison. In 1994 he was inducted into the Country Music Hall of Fame.

Tom Hanks

Tom Hanks (born 1956) is an award-winning actor from Concord, California. His box-office hits include *Splash*, *Big*, *Philadelphia*, *Forrest Gump*, and *Cast Away*. He won Oscars for best actor for *Philadelphia* and *Forrest Gump*.

Steven Jobs (born 1955) and **Steven Wozniak** (born 1950) are business-men who met in Los Altos, California, while working summer jobs at Hewlett-Packard. The two went on to start Apple Computer in Jobs's garage in 1975. The business quickly became one of the largest computer companies in the country.

Steven Jobs

Florence Griffith Joyner (1959–1998) started running at the age of seven in her hometown, Los Angeles. At the 1988 Olympics, she shattered the world record for the 100-meter and the 200-meter dashes and became known as the world's fastest woman.

Jack London (1876–1916), one of the most popular writers of the early 1900s, was born in San Francisco. An adventurer who loved to travel, London followed the gold rush to Canada's Yukon Territory. His most famous book, *The Call of the Wild*, has been translated into more than 50 languages.

Florence Griffith Joyner

Nancy Marie Lopez (born 1957), from Torrance, California, began golfing with her father when she was eight. In 1978 Lopez won five Ladies Professional Golf Association (LPGA) tournaments in a row. She was inducted into the LPGA Hall of Fame in 1987.

George Lucas (born 1944), a film director from Modesto, California, directed the films of the *Star Wars* trilogy. The films were first released in the late 1970s and early 1980s. He updated the special effects and added more scenes in the re-released *Star Wars* films of the mid-1990s.

George Lucas

Marilyn Monroe (1926–1962) was born Norma Jean Baker in Los Angeles. Famous worldwide for her beauty, Monroe starred in several movies, including *Bus Stop*, *The Seven Year Itch*, and *Some Like It Hot*.

Marilyn Monroe

Julia Morgan (1872–1957), an architect from San Francisco, helped rebuild the city after the 1906 earthquake. During her career, Morgan designed more than 700 buildings, including Hearst Castle at San Simeon, California.

Richard Nixon (1913–1994), from Yorba Linda, California, was the 37th president of the United States. Noted for his skill in foreign affairs, Nixon reestablished U.S. relations with China. In 1974, due to his role in the Watergate scandal, he became the first president to resign from office.

Richard Nixon

John Steinbeck (1902–1968) wrote prize-winning stories about the struggles of poor people. His best-known book, *The Grapes of Wrath*, tells the story of migrant workers who move from Oklahoma to California during the Great Depression. Much of Steinbeck's writing is set near his birthplace of Salinas, California.

Yoshiko Uchida (1921–1992), from Alameda, California, wrote stories for children about growing up Japanese American. Her books include *Journey to Topaz*, *The Sea of Gold and Other Tales from Japan*, *Samurai of Gold Hill*, and *Two Foolish Cats*.

John Steinbeck

FACTS-AT-A-GLANCE

Nickname: Golden State

Song: "I Love You, California"

Motto: Eureka ("I've found it")

Flower: California poppy

Tree: California redwood

Bird: California quail

Animal: California grizzly bear (now extinct in California)

Fish: golden trout

Fossil: saber-toothed cat

Gemstone: benitoite

Mineral: gold

Date and ranking of statehood:
September 9, 1850, the 31st state

Capital: Sacramento

Area: 155,973 square miles

Rank in area, nationwide: 3rd

Average January temperature: 44° F

Average July temperature: 75° F

The flag flown during the Bear Flag Revolt was the model for California's state flag. The star represented California's status as an independent republic. The bear served as a warning to the Mexican army that the Californian rebels were willing to fight for freedom.

POPULATION GROWTH

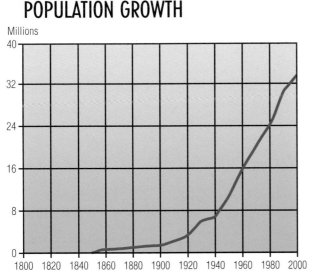

Millions

This chart shows how California's population has grown from 1850 to 2000.

The California state seal was adopted in 1849. The grizzly bear represents California. Next to the bear stands Minerva, the Roman goddess of wisdom. A miner holding a pick represents the mining industry, while grapes and wheat stand for agriculture. The ships represent trade and commerce. The peaks of the Sierra Nevada rise in the background.

Population: 33,871,648 (2000 census)

Rank in population, nationwide: 1st

Major cities and populations: (2000 census) Los Angeles (3,694,820); San Diego (1,223,400); San Jose (894,943); San Francisco (776,733); Long Beach (461,522); Fresno (427,652)

U.S. senators: 2

U.S. representatives: 53

Electoral votes: 55

Natural resources: boron, diatomite, forests, gold, gypsum, natural gas, oil, potash, pumice, sand and gravel, tungsten

Agricultural products: almonds, apricots, avocados, beef cattle, cotton, eggs, grapes, hay, lemons, lettuce, melons, milk, olives, oranges, peaches, pears, plums, strawberries, tomatoes, walnuts

Fishing industry: halibut, herring, mackerel, rockfish, sablefish, salmon, shark, sole, swordfish

Manufactured goods: aircraft, canned fruits and vegetables, cars, computers, hardware, soft drinks, spacecraft, telephone equipment, videotapes, wines

WHERE CALIFORNIANS WORK

Services—67 percent (services include jobs in trade; community, social, and personal services; finance, insurance, and real estate; transportation, communication, and utilities)

Government—13 percent

Manufacturing—11 percent

Construction—5 percent

Agriculture—4 percent

Mining—less than 1 percent

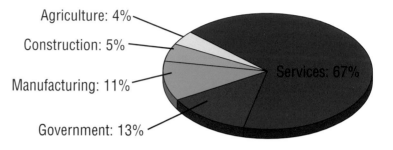

Agriculture: 4%
Construction: 5%
Manufacturing: 11%
Government: 13%
Services: 67%

GROSS STATE PRODUCT

Services—69 percent

Manufacturing—14 percent

Government—11 percent

Construction—3 percent

Agriculture—2 percent

Mining—1 percent

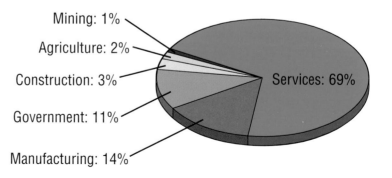

Mining: 1%
Agriculture: 2%
Construction: 3%
Government: 11%
Manufacturing: 14%
Services: 69%

STATE WILDLIFE

Mammals: beaver, bighorn sheep, black bear, cougar, coyote, deer, elephant seal, elk, fox, mink, mountain lion, mountain sheep, muskrat, pronghorn, rabbit, seal, sea lion, sea otter, wildcat, wolverine

Birds: California condor, duck, geese, grouse, mourning dove, peregrine falcon, quail, turkey

Reptiles and amphibians: lizard, rattlesnake, snake, tortoise, turtle

Fish: abalone, black bass, clam, crab, lobster, oyster, salmon, scallop, shrimp, striped bass, trout, whale

Trees: bristlecone pine, cedar, coast redwood, fir, giant sequoia, hemlock, oak, pine, redwood

Wild plants: beardtongue, burroweed, cactus, California poppy, chaparral, creosote bush, desert evening primrose, evening primrose, fiddleneck, fireweed, indigo bush, Joshua tree, lupine, sand verbena, Washington lily

Peregrine falcon

Elephant seals

PLACES TO VISIT

Alcatraz Island, San Francisco
A functioning prison from 1861 until 1963, Alcatraz is located in San Francisco Bay. Its walls once housed Al Capone, "Machine Gun" Kelly, and Robert Franklin Stroud, also known as the "Birdman of Alcatraz."

California missions, California coast
Explore one or more of the 21 religious settlements that span the California coast. Learn how the first Californians of Spanish descent lived, including how they made food and clothing.

Disneyland, Anaheim
The famous amusement park designed by Walt Disney is one of California's most popular attractions.

Hearst Castle, near San Luis Obispo
The former estate of newspaper owner William Randolph Hearst was built like a medieval castle. It houses ancient works of art, and the castle grounds feature a Roman temple.

Knott's Berry Farm, Buena Park
The state's oldest amusement park features rides, a ghost town, and a re-creation of an Indian village.

La Brea Tar Pits, Los Angeles
Located in Hancock Park, the La Brea Tar Pits are a prehistoric graveyard for saber-toothed tigers, giant sloths, and other

creatures. All of these fossils have been preserved in a sticky tar bog. Many skeletons from the bog are on display in the George C. Page Museum.

Marine World/Africa USA, Vallejo

The only combined ocean aquarium and wildlife park in the United States, the park has shows that feature African animals from the sea, land, and air.

Redwood Highway, northern California

Follow U.S. Highway 101 north from San Francisco to Oregon to see some of the tallest living trees in the world.

San Diego Zoo

This zoo is home to three giant pandas from China. Visitors can also see a variety of birds, monkeys, and apes.

Seaworld, San Diego

See Shamu, the killer whale, leap into the air. Also visit manatee, shark, dolphin, and penguin exhibits. Animal shows are scheduled throughout the day.

Universal Studios, Hollywood

Visitors can see how movies are made at the world's largest studio and theme park. A tram whisks visitors through well-known movie sets.

Yosemite National Park, east central California

Waterfalls, giant sequoias, and scenic mountain views make Yosemite one of the most popular national parks in the United States.

ANNUAL EVENTS

Tournament of Roses, Pasadena—*January*

Chinese New Year Celebration, San Francisco and Los Angeles—*January or February*

Return of swallows to San Juan Capistrano—*March*

Cherry Blossom Festival, San Francisco—*April*

Stockton Asparagus Festival, Stockton—*April*

Salinas Valley Fair, King City—*May*

Strawberry Festival, Arroyo Grande—*May*

Garlic Festival, Gilroy—*July*

Old Spanish Days Fiesta, Santa Barbara—*August*

State Fair, Sacramento—*late August–early September*

Monterey Jazz Festival, Monterey—*September*

Black Cowboy Parade, Oakland—*October*

Clam Festival, Pismo Beach—*October*

International Festival of Masks, Los Angeles—*October*

LEARN MORE ABOUT CALIFORNIA

BOOKS

General

Altman, Linda Jacobs. *California*. New York: Marshall Cavendish, 1997. For older readers.

Heinrichs, Ann. *California*. Chicago: Children's Press, 1998. For older readers.

Wills, Charles A. *A Historical Album of California*. Brookfield, CT: Millbrook Press, 1994.

Special Interest

Brown, Tricia. *The City by the Bay: A Magical Journey around San Francisco*. San Francisco: Chronicle Books, 1993. Brown takes the reader to the Golden Gate Bridge, Coit Tower, Mission Delores, the Palace of Fine Arts, and Lombard Street.

California Missions. Minneapolis, MN: Lerner Publications Company, 1996. This six-volume series examines the Spanish mission period of California history. Each volume covers a specific region and features full-color photographs and illustrations.

Dunlap, Julie. *Eye on the Wild: A Story about Ansel Adams*. Minneapolis, MN: Carolrhoda Books, Inc., 1995. A biography of the world-famous nature photographer and conservationist, who was born in San Francisco.

Jaskol, Julie, and Brian Lewis. *City of Angels: In and Around Los Angeles.* New York: Dutton, 1999. Readers tour sights in the Los Angeles area, including Chinatown, Hollywood, La Brea Tar Pits, the farmers' market, and Watts Towers.

Lee, Georgia. *A Day with a Chumash.* Minneapolis, MN: Runestone Press, 1999. Combines facts and fiction to tell the story of life in a Chumash village.

Thompson, Sharon Elaine. *Death Trap: The Story of the La Brea Tar Pits.* Minneapolis, MN: Lerner Publications Company, 1994. Thompson describes the digging of fossils at the La Brea Tar Pits in Los Angeles. Find out how the tar pits formed and why animals became trapped there. For older readers.

Fiction

Cushman, Karen. *The Ballad of Lucy Whipple.* New York: Clarion Books, 1996. Twelve-year-old Lucy Whipple moves with her family to California from Massachusetts in 1849. She copes with her new life in a rough mining town.

Lowell, Susan. *I Am Lavina Cumming.* Minneapolis, MN: Milkweed Editions, 1993. After 10-year-old Lavina's mother dies, she goes to live with relatives in California. While she's there, the great San Francisco earthquake strikes.

West, Tracey. *Fire in the Valley.* New York: Silver Moon Press, 1993. Twelve-year-old Sarah writes a letter to President Theodore Roosevelt to protest diverting water from her family's farm for use by the growing city of Los Angeles.

WEBSITES

Welcome to California
<http://www.state.ca.us/>
California's official website offers information about the state
government, state organizations, and a variety of state services.
Links to other California-related sites are also provided.

California Travel and Tourism
<http://gocalif.ca.gov/>
The California Division of Tourism provides facts, photographs,
maps, and other travel ideas to travelers in California.

Los Angeles Times
<http://latimes.com>
Read about current events in southern California and the world in
this online version of the *Los Angeles Times.*

The San Francisco Chronicle
<http://www.sfgate.com/chronicle>
Follow events in northern California and the world by reading the
online version of this nationally known newspaper.

PRONUNCIATION GUIDE

Cabrillo, Juan Rodríguez (kah-BREE-yoh, hwahn rohth-REE-gayth)

Chumash (CHOO-mash)

Cinco de Mayo (SINK-oh day MY-oh)

Monterey (mahn-tuh-RAY)

San Diego (san dee-AY-goh)

San Francisco (san fran-SIHS-koh)

San Joaquin (san wah-KEEN)

San Jose (san ho-ZAY)

Santa Cruz (sant-uh KROOZ)

Serra, Junípero (SEHR-rah, hoo-NEE-peh-roh)

Sierra Nevada (see-AYR-uh nuh-VA-duh)

Yosemite (yoh-SEHM-uh-tee)

San Franciscans call this part of Lombard Street the "crookedest street in the world."

GLOSSARY

desert: an area of land that receives only about 10 inches or less of rain or snow a year

fault line: a break in the earth's crust where one side has moved up or down so that it no longer matches the other side. Earthquakes occur along fault lines.

fossil fuel: a material such as coal or oil that is formed in the earth from the remains of ancient plants and animals. Fossil fuels are used to produce power.

glacier: a large body of ice and snow that moves slowly over land

immigrant: a person who moves into a foreign country and settles there

irrigation: a method of watering land by directing water through canals, ditches, pipes, or sprinklers

Latino: a person living in the United States who either came from or has ancestors from Latin America. Latin America includes Mexico and most of Central and South America.

mission: a place where missionaries work. Missionaries are people sent out by a religious group to spread its beliefs to other peoples.

peninsula: a stretch of land almost completely surrounded by water

smog: a heavy haze that forms in the air when smoke and fog combine

strait: a narrow stretch of water that connects two larger bodies of water

treaty: an agreement between two or more groups, usually having to do with peace or trade

INDEX

PHOTO ACKNOWLEDGMENTS

Cover photographs by © Michael T. Sedam/CORBIS, front (left), spine and back cover; © Robert Landau/CORBIS, front (right). PresentationMaps.com, pp. 1, 8, 9, 51; © Galen Rowell/CORBIS, pp. 2–3; © Stuart Westmorland/CORBIS, p. 3; © David Muench/CORBIS, pp. 4 (detail), 7 (detail, left), 19 (detail, left), 42 (detail), 54 (detail); © Tom Bean, p. 6; Bonnie J. Fisher, p. 7 (right); Diane Cooper, p. 10; Saul Mayer, pp. 11 (left), 26; Frederica Georgia, pp. 11 (right), 48 (left); Nancy Hoyt Belcher, pp. 12, 43 (left & right), 45, 47 (both), 49; © Kenneth W. Fink/Root Resources, p. 13; © Bill Varie/CORBIS, p. 14; Library of Congress, pp. 15, 38; © Ted Spiegel/CORBIS, p. 16; David E. Trask/Laatsch-Hupp Photo, p. 17; © Alan G. Nelson/Root Resources, p. 18; Santa Barbara Museum of Natural History, p. 19 (right); Bancroft Library, pp. 20, 22, 24, 25, 35; Laura Westlund, p. 21; © Bettmann/CORBIS, pp. 28, 37, 41, 56; © James L. Amos/CORBIS, p. 29; © Robert Holmes/CORBIS, p. 31; Tim Seeley, pp. 32, 63, 71, 72; CA State Railroad Museum, p. 34; Coll. of the Santa Barbara Historical Museums, p. 36; © Horace Bristol/COR-BIS, p. 39; © Shmuel Thaler, pp. 43 (center), 57, 58, 73 (top); © Mark E. Gibson/CORBIS, p. 44; © AFP/CORBIS, p. 46; Betty Groskin, p. 48 (right); Doyen Salsig, p. 50 (left); © Vince Streano/CORBIS, p. 50 (right); © James Blank/Root Resources, p. 52; © Nik Wheeler/CORBIS, p. 55; Gene Ahrens, p. 60; © Richard Cummins/CORBIS, p. 61; © Craig Lovell/CORBIS, p. 66 (top); City of L.A., p. 66 (second from top); Hollywood Book & Poster, pp. 66 (second from bottom), 67 (bottom), 69 (second from top); © Mitchell Gerber/CORBIS, pp. 66 (bottom), 68 (second from top); New York Yankees, p. 67 (top); © Rufus F. Folkks/CORBIS, p. 67 (second from top); © Hulton-Deutsch Collection/CORBIS, p. 67 (second from bottom); Concert Express, p. 68 (top); © Reuters NewMedia Inc./CORBIS, pp. 68 (second from bottom), 69 (top); © Neal Preston/CORBIS, p. 68 (bottom); © Ted Streshinsky/CORBIS, p. 69 (second from bottom); National Archives, Neg. No. 306-PS-C.59-11258, p. 69 (bottom); Jean Matheny, p. 70 (top); © Anthony Mercieca/Root Resources, p. 73 (bottom); Henry J. Hupp/Laatsch-Hupp Photo, p. 80.